The Ghosts of Our Words Will Be Heroes in Hell

Poems by

The NÜ Profits of P/o-/e/t/i/c DiSchord

OAC BOOKS
OSAGE ARTS COMMUNITY

OAC Books
Belle, MO
osageac.org

Copyright © Jason Ryberg, Damian Rucci,
John Dorsey, Victor Clevenger, 2020
First Edition: 1 3 5 7 9 10 8 6 4 2
ISBN: 978-1-952411-25-0
LCCN: 2020941915

Cover and author photos: Victor Clevenger
All rights reserved. No part of this publication may be
reproduced or transmitted in any form or by any means,
electronic or mechanical, including photocopying,
recording or by info retrieval system, without prior
written permission from the author.

Acknowledgments:

Jason Ryberg: Special thanks to El Dopa, John T. Keehan, Jr., Jon Lee Grafton, Will Leathem, Namoi Shupp-Pavey, Damian Rucci, John Dorsey, Victor Clevenger, Mark McClane, Tony Hayden and the Osage Arts Community and the Aaron Morrison Home for Wayward Middle-Aged Men.

Damian Rucci: Thank you to the editors of *As It Ought To Be Magazine, Daily Drunk Magazine, Winedrunk Sidewalk, Cultural Weekly, Emerging Lit Journal, Black Coffee Review, Wine Cellar Press, No Contact Magazine, Maverick Duck Press,* and P*unk Provincial Press* where some of these poems originally appeared. Thank you to my supporters who keep me going and Rebecca, who without her love these poems wouldn't exist.

John Dorsey: Special thanks to Mark McClane & Tony Hayden of Osage Arts Community, where all of these poems were created, for their continued generous support, as well as the following supporters, editors and publications, Ray Swaney from *Ted Ate America*, D.R. Wagner Co-Editor of *Quiet Rooms*, Adrian Belmes from Badlung Press, Jay Miner from the *Rustbelt Review*, Chase Dimock from *As It Ought to Be Magazine*, Rebecca Schumejda & Daniel Crocker from the *The Trailer Park Quarterly*, & S.A.Griffin from *MEAT*, as well as Mike & Eva West, Jocelyne Desforges, David A. Pratt, Matthew Shaw, Lois McClure-Smith, Larry Gawel, John Clayton, David E. Oprava, Steve Goldberg, Cristin Hemingway Jaynes, Bradford Middleton, Jason Shelley, Pete Donohue, Jeff & Tobi Alfier, Victor Clevenger & Crissy Staton, & all of my subscribers.

Victor Clevenger: Special Thanks is given to Crissy Staton, Jason Baldinger, Curtis Hayes, Wendy Rainey, Linzi Garcia, Jase Buck, Mark McClane, Tony Hayden, Matthew Haines, Taylor Teachout, Jeremy Gulley, Michelle Willis, Carlie Clevenger, Cassie Clevenger, The Milkman, & S.A. Griffin.

TABLE OF CONTENTS

Jason Ryberg

Open Letter to Lucas Jackson / 1

Wherein It Conquers the World / 2

Whatever It Was / 4

Consolation Prize / 5

Portrait of Old Man Smoking Cigarettes
   and Drinking Beer While Listening to the
   Cardinals / Royals Game on the Radio / 6

Grandeur / 7

Just Like That / 8

My Shoes, My Belt or My Haircut
   Never Got Me Laid / 10

LA-Z-BOY on the Front Porch / 12

Death Motif / 13

Your Sacrifices Are Greatly Appreciated / 15

Still-Life of Pocket Knife, Carpenter's Pencil
   and Black Velvet Elvis / 16

The Kind of Weed / 17

Preoccupied / 18

Gas Station Famous / 19

The Imp of the Perverse / 21

A Grand Old Time / 22

Beef, It's What's for Dinner! / 23

Dreams of Empty Houses / 24

All the Points of the Compass / 25

Damian Rucci

In the Foothills of the Ozarks / 29

Billboards Over Kansas / 30

I Want to Be a Good Man But / 32

Send It / 33

When You're Poor / 35

Jesus Can Wait / 37

In Places Like This / 39

Missouri I Hope I Never See You Again / 41

Padgett's Pool Hall At Noon / 43

Work Haiku / 44

Good Morning Iran / 46

Suburban Meditation / 49

But When I Get Clean Baby / 51

Most Days / 53

John Dorsey

Anything with Feathers / 57

You Can't Get Blood from the Dead / 59

Greg Before the Fall of the Berlin Wall / 60

Annette is Always with You / 61

The Prettiest Girl in La Junta, Colorado / 62

The Ballad of Mick Ronson / 63

Crystal / 64

Flashlight Neon Light / 65

Color Theory in the Summer of 1980 / 66
Radio Cities & Number One Records / 68
Wrestling With the Bear / 69
The Finger Has Got to Come Off / 70
Jason Baldinger Talks About the Future / 71
Perpetual Motion / 72
As Curtis Drives By / 74
Greg's Mantra / 75
Detroit Airport in Route to London / 76
Detroit Airport in Route to London #2 / 77
Poem for Damian Rucci / 78
At the Venture Hostel / 79
Beth Saves My Life / 80
Poem for Winston Trew / 81

Victor Clevenger

Poem for My Grandson / 85
Southern Un-Hospitality / 86
2 Lovers on South Aiken Avenue / 87
What I Didn't Know While Eating Bacon
    in Jeannette, Pennsylvania / 88
Three Minutes Late & Out of Luck / 89
The Color of a Deep Depression / 90
Lost Man's Candle / 92
Poem for My Hometown (or,
    An Abusive Relationship) / 93

Poem for Lora / 94

A Poem About Rose Bushes / 95

Poem for Carlie & Cassie Clevenger / 97

Clevenger Painting / 98

I am Legend (or, Poem About Helping My
   Children Build Valentine's Day Boxes) / 99

Poem for Madi / 100

Jay / 101

Jay #2 / 102

Jay #3 / 103

Jay #4 / 104

Jay #5 / 105

Favorite Couch at the Dorsey Hotel / 106

Southern Missouri Hindsight Proverb / 108

Reggie & The Milkman / 109

the promise of lightning is
that all poets die empty

and the ghosts of their words
will be heroes in hell

-Victor Alan Smith

Jason Ryberg

Open Letter to Lucas Jackson

You sad sack of new meat, you.
You beheader of parking meters, you.
You malicious destroyer of municipal properties.
You unrecognizable pup.
You failure as a communicator, you,
    back-sasser, box-dweller,
    rabbit blood, hog gut.
You tireless devourer of eggs, you.
You kicker of bucks, you.
You chain-buster, gun-fetcher,
    natural-born world-shaker.
You back roads swamp-runner.
You good ol' boy.
You cool, cool
    big beautiful handful
    of nothing, you.

Laugh it up, kid.

May your mind never
be right.

Wherein *It* Conquers the World

It rolls with the punchlines
and bends like a skinny tree in the wind
to that point just before snapping.

It tips its hat to the ladies,
tips the scales in favor of the little man,
tip-toes off the tip of your tongue and swan-dives
out into the blue, wide-open market place of ideas.

It curves, effortlessly, into the helical turning of
glow worms and screw-guns, the pyrning and gyring
of falcons on the horizon and cop-copters circling,
ominously, above your neighborhood.

It will drop some knowledge on your dumb ass,
drop a grand in a weekend like it's nothing but it will
never, ever drop a dime on anyone for anything.

It pounds and pounds on the door
at the top of the high stairwell of night,
demanding an audience with whoever
is in charge of this clusterfuck shit-show.

It carries water, chops wood, carries more water,
chops more wood, all with the hope of attaining
enlightenment, as in that big *E* Enlightenment.

It folds the space / time continuum from time to time
in order to bring two seemingly disparate points
of view together.

It occasionally uses a bit of information to chisel
a few bucks, here and there, just enough to scrape
together bus fair and beer money.

It lifts the truth up on high
then casts it down from the mountaintop,
tears it up, tears it down, builds it all up again
from the foundation to the stars.

It resides somewhere between *plausible deniability*
and *terminological inexactitude,* that sweet spot
between the unwavering constant and the ever-
shifting variable.

It's the broom in the corner,
the tractor hibernating in the barn,
the glowing tip of the hermit's cigar.

It's the sun pooling on the tree-line,
the blue moon in the window,
the classified section of a foreign newspaper
blowing along the docks in an icy grey wind.

It's the futile and eternal dog-tail chase for truth
(or its nearly-identical twin, at least), down and down
the spiraling / corkscrew snake hole
of ever-diminishing returns.

Whatever It Was

You know,
I'd think twice
about fuckin' around
with that thing
if I was you
said the old man
with the the eye-patch
and prosthetic limb,
as he eyeballed us, hairily,
from his back porch swing
with his one good orb,
looking like some
mad Ahab type dude
that, one day back in
the who knows when,
had just washed ashore
and never left.
But we all shrugged
and went on poking it
with our sticks.
Whatever it
was.

Consolation Prize

There was a part of me that, all these years later, still really wanted to read her the riot act, to give her the old *what for* and inform her that the faded lavender bandana she gave me back then (to remember her by, I guess, or as some kind of bullshit consolation prize, maybe, for not *qualifying*, hell, for not even being considered a contender or even a valid, bona fide practitioner of the sport, that same bandana that had, so often, tweaked me, existentially, from time to time, over the years, whenever it would randomly resurface to remind me how much she had hooked me and how I had barely registered with her), well, it was hanging from the rear-view mirror of my buddy's primer-gray pick-up truck and he and it were halfway to Denver by now. But what would the damn point of such a petty little gesture even be? We hadn't spoken in close to twenty years. She wouldn't know what I was talking about because there never had been a *me and her*. Just me—carrying around the fallen baby bird of a wounded ego and the whole *what might have been* syndrome all this time, thinking that somehow, somewhere down the line we'd run into each other again. Hell, she probably wouldn't even remember my name.

Portrait of Old Man Smoking Cigarettes and Drinking Beer While Listening to the Cardinals / Royals Game on the Radio
for George McLane

A lampshade (looking, somehow, like a colorful,
wide-brimmed gaucho's hat, complete with dangly
tassles, even) hanging from the ceiling by an ornate
chain, its 60-watt bulb illuminating a kitchen table
where an old man wearing a St. Louis Cardinal's cap
sits smoking the stub of a cigarette while pulling
a fresh one from a crumpled softpack of Chesterfields,
pouring Busch beer from a can into a wineglass
from which he sips between deep drags and
disconcerting fits of hacking and coughing,
a Cardinals / Royals game crackling from an old
Phillips pocket transistor radio *(21 to 14, Cardinals),*
and, over there in the corner, amongst all the dust
and spider webs and boxes packed full of who
the hell knows what, as if it had been censured
and banished for merely trying to do its job,
an oxygen tank on wheels, an oxygen tank
that if it had a face, would have a sour,
disapproving look on it.

Grandeur

The sky was the
whole panoramic
spectrum assortment
of Crayola reds,
oranges, yellows
and purples—
a pinata ripped
wide-open like
a giant ten-
point buck
by the side
of the road,
soaked with
gasoline
and lit with
a blue tip
match, and we
nothing more
than madly
scrambling ants
beneath its hot
and bloody
grandeur.
Or at least
that's the way
it seemed
to me
that
day.

Just Like That

This trippy old dude
always going on and on
to himself (or anybody else
he could catch away from
the safety of the herd and
skillfully maneuver into a
corner of his never-ending
conference-call with the
universe) about butterflies,
butterflies, butterflies,
his shabby shotgun shack
(down there where the
tracks used to run before
the *government or who-the-
hell-ever* ripped them up,
years ago, *so's the trains
can't ever come back*)
full of cages of butterflies,
books about butterflies,
VHS and DVDs on
how to attract butterflies,
how to raise butterflies,
how to rebuild entire
butterfly habitats, even,
and the whole house and yard
saturated damn-near down
to the sub-atomic level with
the velvety, lover-like
flitter and slap of butterfly

wings, like this guy
had some kind of
supernatural pact with
the god (or most likely,
goddess) of butterflies,
and then one day,
while walking down
the street, pontificating,
no doubt, upon his
favorite topic, did, suddenly,
according to at least one
(mostly sober) eye-witness,
go POOF into a million
multi-colored wings
and was gone,
just like
that.

My Shoes, My Belt or My Haircut Never Got Me Laid

for Steve Bridgens

Got no fancy gilded pot to piss in
or bay window over-looking some
majestic scene to throw it out of.

Got no antique grandfather clock
to tell me what time it is,

no Teddy Roosevelt-ian moustache
or Walt Whitman-esque beard to express
my ironic sense of masculinity.

Got no basement full of home-brewed
and bottled cases of beer or wine made from
weeds and wildflowers from my backyard,

no Eurotrash wanna-be or fashionista-like
need to see or be seen making the scene,
no need to primp, preen, vogue and parade
my boheme credentials (beta-minus, at best).

I have no shame or need to defend my belief
in the profound depths, nuances and complexities
of an expertly crafted vanilla ice cream.

Though I will admit that when I occasionally
saunter and carouse about the town,
(a Hammond B3 and stand-up bass in my head
and my roving and curious eyes hidden behind
a cheap pair of shades), it is understandable
how I might be confused for a member of the *tribe*.

But really, I'm just doing my best
to make it from point A to B to C
(as inconspicuously incognito as I can be),
all the while avoiding the twin dueling
guard tower spots of Melodramatic Intrigue
and Law Enforcement, alike,

my mind fixed, less and less, these days,
it seems, on social media networking
or chance romantic encounters
and more and more on just
making my way home
(relatively unscathed),
one last drink,
a few chapters
from a book, maybe,
and an early bed.

LA-Z-BOY on the Front Porch

Reading lamp to the left. ☑

Side table with book and expertly crafted
    Manhattan or Old Fashioned to the right. ☑

Christmas lights left up year 'round and blazing
    like constellations of fireflies. ☑

Radio somewhere tuned to the classical station
    (currently featuring a solo for piano by Domenico
    Scarlatti, or one of that crew). ☑

The traffic and dogs around town mostly
    settled down for the night. ☑

The wind stirring the trees up a bit, here and there,
    but nothing to get too excited about. ☑

My God, it's all so fucking civilized.

Death Motif

I have often envisioned Death as a bullet
from a gun in the hand of some dumb *fuckemo*
sticking up a Quick Trip at 1am who has decided,
suddenly, that he just doesn't like the looks of me.

I have envisioned Death as a pale, riderless horse,
without warning and for no reason apparent to me,
kicking my brains into next week.

I have envisioned Death as a carving knife plunged
into my pumpkin-like head by a woman who has finally
reached her point of critical mass with me.

I have envisioned death as a twenty car pile-up
on an iced-over highway late at night.

I have envisioned Death as an airplane suddenly
stripping a gear or throwing a rod and free-falling
into the ocean.

I have envisioned Death as haplessly bobbing
along somewhere at sea and waiting for one or more
of its inhabitants to take an interest in me.

I have envisioned Death as the edge of a thirty-story
building urging me toward it with my own morbid
curiosity.

I have envisioned Death as the gaping and jagged maw
of a Grizzly Bear suddenly appearing in my path
on a leisurely stroll through a landscape where
Grizzly Bears have never been reported.

Death as slow-motion, mutually assured
nuclear destruction.

Death as inbred mutant psycho with chainsaw,
shotgun or fire-axe.

Death as incurable disease or serious injury
and me just another one of the 1/3 of Americans
without any health insurance or savings.

Death as a serious misunderstanding between me
and a SWAT team kicking my door in
at 4 in the morning.

But, as a matter of fact, I have never, ever pictured or
dreamed of Death as hooded grim reaper-type character
or devilishly dapper dude at the wheel of a hearse,
patiently waiting for me to get my affairs in order.

Your Sacrifices Are Greatly Appreciated

It is no great secret that the unrequited needs and desires of low-status drones (and all other various sub-stratum of ineligible walk-ons and aspiring would-be suitor types) are routinely and ritually tossed into the gaping maw of Love's not quite always roaring and never quite extinct volcano, as pre-emptive deterrent for any future uppity and insolent attempts at unchecked upward social / sexual mobility by the unwashed riff-raff from the general admission section, but also as genuine sacrificial offering to whatever dark gods who might be swayed into positively influencing the probability of another bountiful crop of beautiful rich babies as well as functioning as another buffer layer of assurance that the hopes and dreams and genes of the more desireable members of the hive are more fully realized and propagated. Surely, you can understand this, and your sacrifices are greatly appreciated. Truly, they are.

Still-Life of Pocket Knife, Carpenter's Pencil and Black Velvet Elvis

There was a wadded-up brown paper bag (with a few phone numbers and some directions hastily scrawled upon it), a brass candle-holder shaped like a chess piece (a king or queen, maybe, but the wax of many multi-colored candles had melted down over it, over the years, rendering it mostly gender-neutral, by now) and a set of keys that looked as if they unlocked massive doors and gates and gothic trunks and chests best left unopened, all arranged on an ancient card table (the kind you always got stuck at every goddamn Thanksgiving as far back as you can remember), a man, snoring, steadily, in a kicked-back La-Z-Boy chair in front of a Red Wings / Black Hawks game, a coffee mug of Diet Coke and bourbon, balanced precariously, on his slowly rising / slowly falling / slowly rising / slowly falling belly, (bloated with what appears to be most of an Imo's meat lover's pizza), a pocket-knife covered in red sauce and cheese, and the stub of a carpenter's pencil permanently fixed behind his left ear. A black velvet Elvis wearing gold wrap-around shades watches over it all and keeps him safe.

The Kind of Weed

that gets you to thinking that even though you've been drinking beer, off and on, since about noon (but hell, beer ain't really drinking, is it, now?) and even though it's been about 97+ degrees most of the day, and you've been out in it laboring away with your buddy, swabbing his house some godawful shade of atomic pea soup vomit green, still, a couple hits of this stuff after you've called it quits for the day has you, suddenly, reinvigorated and fairly confident that you can make it through all of the *Lord of the Rings* or *Matrix* trilogy tonight, maybe order some pizzas and invite some folks over, but the next thing you know is you've woken from what seems like multiple lifetimes' worth of the weirdest dreams you've ever dreamed: dreams as real and crystal freaking clear as your Hi-Def TV screen, here, dreams as freaky as any movie you've ever seen, dreams just a little too Freudian and Jungian to go into too much detail, here, concerning, and it must be almost dawn and you're sitting upright in the middle of the couch, clothes and shoes still on, a nearly full beer in your hand, tilted, slightly (at whatever windmill that has most recently appeared on the horizon of your mind) but still remaining somehow unspilled, a movie paused on the TV, and somewhere, birds starting to sing.

Preoccupied

She's the only woman I've ever known
who ever said she loved me,

and she said it all the time,

though never quite so earnestly
as when she was lamenting
the latest disappointing *boy-de-jour,*
(only just recently pulled from the
ever-turning hotdog rotisserie
of indistinguishable
softboi / art-school types),

the only one who really hooked
the old battleship chain
and two-ton anchor
to the base of my spine,

upon which she would (unwittingly,
no doubt) tap out a seemingly meaningless
Morse code of sexual polyrhythms,
from time to time,
when she wasn't otherwise
preoccupied with something
more engaging.

Gas Station Famous
for Victor Clevenger and John Dorsey

It was a Neo-Western movie of a hot and windy
Saturday morning in mid-September and summer was
clearly letting us know that it wasn't quite done with us yet.

We were buying coffee and donuts and DayQuil at a
gas station just outside of St. John, Kansas in a desperate,
pre-emptive effort to circumnavigate our looming
collective hangovers before they really kicked in.

I was wearing all black, doing my best working-man chic /
third-rate Tom Waits / Mike Ness shtick: big boots,
big belt buckle and paper-boy hat (rakishly angled).

Victor had more of a quaffed and groomed punk rock /
hip-hop thing going; red Chuck Taylors, baggy jeans,
a black stingy-brim and silk bowling style shirt showing
his sleeves of tattoos, plus just the faintest hint of cologne.

And John was just *doing John* as only John can do:
golden ringlets and big, bushy Walt Whitman / Taliban beard
(a few grains of powdered sugar here and there), classic
black-rimmed Buddy Holly / nerd glasses (with the obligatory
bit of duct tape to hold the whole shaky framework together),
and Doc Marten's with Virgin Marys painted on them.

It's possible we may have appeared a bit *exotic* and *outlandish*
to some of the locals who came and went with their purchases
that morning: *not from around here* written all over us:

and the three of us just sitting there, on the bench outside,
sipping our coffee, scratching away at lottery tickets,
trying to figure out our next move while watching a lone
tumbleweed drunkenly meander its way North on US 281.

Every now and then a car or truck would slow way down
to check us out, make a u-turn in the parking lot then
drive by again.

Hell, maybe they wanted to kick our weirdo, beatnik asses.
Maybe they didn't want our *type* in their town.
Or, maybe we just had the up-all-night / hangover /
caffiene / paranoia blues. You never know.

But we had no time for that foolishness, anyhow.
We needed pancakes and bacon, greasy, runny eggs
and coffee, always more coffee. We were *on tour!*

That meant a solid week on the road and off the grid—
three vagabond, lowbrow *bon-vivant* Quixotes of poesy—
AWOL, MIA and *current whereabouts unknown,*
spreading the seed of The Word wherever the wind took us...

Eventually, the girl working there came outside,
fired up a Pall Mall and asked us,

Y'all famous?

The Imp of the Perverse

You would think that at this stage of the game one would have their business together enough, at least, in regards to the basics of maintenance and general upkeep, risk assessment and impulse control, but no, the ability to momentarily let one's judgment drift askew and make bad decisions is bone deep and muscle memorized, most likely mixed into the very ink in which the sacred script of the DNA is written, and no matter how much cognitive therapy you've had or how many years it's been since your last *incident*, you know your old road dog / runnin' buddy from way back will always be there, waiting for you to call.

A Grand Old Time

Last night
the moon made me get up
from my kitchen table and
my cracked bone china mug
of herbal tea, put on my coat
and my hat, walk out the
back door and wander off
into the hills to run with my
wild cousins, the coyotes,
through fields and backyards
and gardens, howling, yipping
and generally laughing it up,
having a grand old time of it all,
with no thoughts of tomorrow,
when suddenly the sun
began creeping up over
the distant tree line
and told us all
to get on
home.

Beef, It's What's for Dinner!

The wind is whipping up
little cyclones of dust and leaves
in the ditch by the side of Old 40 HWY,

and there's a star-shine gleam
to the chrome ball-hitch
of the pick-up truck in front of me,

and there's road-side fences to the future,
telephone poles to the past,

and the sun, like a cyclop's murder-red eye
is climbing up from behind the horizon
and right into my driver's-side
rear-view mirror,

and *Walk, Don't Run* by the Ventures
is playing now on the radio

and there, above it all,
a lone falcon or hawk sits, calmly,
surveying its little fiefdom from the top
of a billboard sign that reads,

Beef, it's what's for dinner!

You got that right, pal.

Dreams of Empty Houses

Time is always calling
or dropping by (without calling)
at all the wrong goddamn times,

always unexpectedly just coming around
and turning up at the absolutely most
inconvenient and inappropriate moments,

inviting itself in and over-staying its welcome,
bumming all your cigarettes and beers,
using up the minutes on your phone and finally

leaving you, this time, with nothing but
a useless ring of keys, a head full of
crack-pot schemes, a vague sense of having
forgotten or misplaced something, and,

for some strange reason, dreams of empty
houses and apartments where you just can't
be sure you've ever been in, let alone
maybe even lived once.

All the Points of the Compass
with apologies to Tom Stoppard

You could be one of those
John D. Rockefeller types
with interest, credit and dividends
to burn, and legions of laborers
and company men yoked to each
gilded coach like Clydesdales or
Lipizzaner stallions,

you could be a rogue, romantic Jedi
or irresistably charming bandit prince
of poets somehow defying all known
universal laws regarding the natural
and equitable distribution of the world's
singularly sweetest fruit,

you could be Otis, the town drunk,
a low-rent Li Po, shuffling, belching
and farting away your days in poetic
Nirvanish glee down the plum blossom-
lined streets of the quaint little Mayberry, USA
of your wine-soaked mind—

*and for all the points of the compass,
there is only one direction and time
is its only measure*, and it's only a matter
of time before you're carried calmly out to
(or paddling madly backwards from)
the roaring falls of the Great Unknown.

Damian Rucci

In the Foothills of the Ozarks

An American flag
a Midwestern love song

a six-gun salute
in a muddy river bed

the skeletons of the Osage
run naked and free
skip rocks down the Gasconade

the daughters of farmers
cut their hair short
find agency in their bones

live their truths
in gay bars in big cities
never to return to their
barn shaped prisons

on the foothills of the Ozarks
everything is magic
music swims in the blood
of the porch sitters

Billboards Over Kansas

Billboards over Kansas fields
Are you on your way to Heaven?
we're sweating in this car
six hours out from Missouri
waiting to break out into dry heat

we're not on our way to heaven
only to Salina, only to
grab a fist full of America
the bars are already filled
with men who have never tried
so we head for the highways

back home, our old friends
are tucking their children to sleep
are singing lullabies to future senators
but Emery has some couches downstairs
and tomorrow is a myth we're unsure of

on Sante Fe Avenue, at the bookstore
we read poems for local drunks & kids,
cop cheap blotter acid and tiptoe
through the headstone reveries to Kwik Shop
solace can only be found in these moments

but dawn will find us writing poems
in someone else's backyard
with the sleep still caught in our eyes
we pack the car and leave for Texas
never thinking to look back at home

I Want to Be a Good Man But

I would trade my soul for a bag of groceries
to watch you fill your belly with sweetness
by the time the store clerk calls the police
the meal will be in the oven, our lives will be
saved, if God forgives than he will forgive me
and all the sins it took for us to reach him

Send It

He who packs the bong sends
it off with a column of smoke
if it yellows, if the cloud escapes
then that sonofabitch gave a full send

It's all about the ritual; a circle
the glass passes between warm
hands, finger tips briefly meeting
how long can we hold this down,

down here? Before we're torn away
by the pestilences of the outside world
the hopes that keep us going, the faces
it's easier to forget, hallelujah, none of it

matters, we're columns of atoms
vibrating too fast but this'll ground us
this will keep our feet tucked into the carpet
the smoke dances between loose lips

If Jesus ever spoke, then he spoke in
moments like these tucked away
in the apartments of the faithless
echoed down lonely hallways

the only church I've ever known
is here now, trading smoke with you
coughing our passage to those holy gates
and one day all of this will be gone

When You're Poor

when you're poor
you're always fucking
or fighting

always fucking because there
is never anything to do
but thrust & moan

when that's done
then you're fighting
fighting to keep the lights on

fighting to keep the bills paid
fighting to find change to do the laundry
& fighting with the landlord
about that fifty bucks
he's still missing

but it could be worse
you could always be waiting again
waiting for the electricity company
to finally kill the lights

waiting for that check to hit
the mail box
waiting for the winds to blow
luck your way for once

Jesus Can Wait

I can't believe
what you told me tonight
that we came out here
to clean up and see the sun
for once, but it's two am
naked on a three-day bender

sniffing speed off of Crowley books
as if railing powdered magic can save us
as if we were born for this
as if the sins of our fathers
painted yellow brick roads to addiction

there's always someone on our front porch
either our junkie neighbor or a savior
you know I'm only letting one of them in
Jesus can wait, the devil isn't known to be patient

the monsters get you in your dreams
and that's why I never go to sleep
stay up with me baby, one more night
Jesus will be there in the morning

the outside will be there in the morning
the world can wait for us, don't worry

my horoscopes are highways
to oblivion so save the Hallmark cards for
a soul worth saving

can you give me a minute?
someone's knocking on the door

In Places Like This

In places like this
   you can almost hear
   the heartland love songs
the other night, someone's
   baby daddy raced the devil
   down route 28 and lost
   his motorcycle bent into
   an obelisk outside the supermarket
   a monument to a moment
   now eclipsed by sorrow

In places like this
   the buffalo no longer roam
   instead they circle the skies
   as pensive white clouds
   bringing rain down on
   brimmed hats of farmers
   their children smoke marijuana
   hunt for the cool glow
   of urban rebellion, the distant
   horns of longing fade in the foothills

In places like this
   we dance along the gravel country roads
   in the beds of pickup trucks

with the lights out so we can watch
the galaxy spin above our heads
watch the gods sway in celestial winds
cheap beer, our sacrament to nirvana
or whatever destination awaits us all
in the dark

In places like this
  I am a ghost

Missouri I Hope I Never See You Again

Missouri

I hope I never see you again
or at least, that part of you
dirty and anxious outside the gas station

I hope I never see
your barefoot children
running through my dreams
pockets full of roses and crystal

I have followed them down
the country roads through the creeks
to vacant barns and broken light bulbs
to my neighbor's kitchen table

I hope I never see the serpent
of smoke that slithers from
a tin-foil boat and finds its home
in the chasm where my soul

once lived but has gone on vacation
has packed up his suitcases
and tore off for Rolla airport
I may never see him again

I hope I never see your
red lit sinister streets, the shadows
panhandling outside of the supermarket
the damned rotting at the motel

from the rear-view mirror
I watch my neighbor fight
an invisible foe, by the time
he calls for help we're on
an interstate highway
and the only way to look
is ahead

Padgett's Pool Hall At Noon

all the best joints let you smoke
while you're drinking

each pitcher is a milestone to nirvana
two in and the afternoon is bright
four and the dogs come out of the men

the truth hangs on loose lips
love is a commodity that hangs on a moment

and where are you now?
the noon drink has become a marathon
the boys have dropped their hats
character fades in the beer foam

the Missouri sky waves goodnight
and we've killed a keg in conversation
the night calls us elsewhere
and you aren't here
and you aren't here

Work Haiku

A soda machine
humming; clock that no longer
clicks, work man's solace

if they only knew
how much time I spent right here
texting on the john

they would cut me loose
write me up, dim yellow lights
far out now on the couch

but destitute broke
somewhere I'll never return
to, I'll get up now

shake these stubborn legs
to life, find my aisle
open tired eyes

one day I'll be free
to roam from coast to coast, but
there's no free lunch what

you take must be paid
for in blood or worse in time
I know I'll be back

once the road's asleep
when the birds stop singing Spring
choruses for me

and in this storefront
I will pack out groceries
eyes on the highway

Good Morning Iran

Good morning Iran

it's Friday, eleven pm
my streets are quiet yet vibrant
the weekend is blooming over Manhattan
its lights are a halo across the Hudson

it's morning in Shiraz
the weak winter sun
paints the Persian Gulf golden
I watch you from
seven thousand miles away

you're another foreign target
to be crossed out
like Iraq
like Libya
like Afghanistan
you don't want to play with atoms
do you know what it feels like
to vaporize seventy thousand lives?
Do you know what it feels like
to play God?

Good morning Iran
I see your militias outside of Aleppo
trying to push the rebels to sea
have you seen mine?

Have you seen Uncle Sam's artillery
firing shells from the rubble of Homs?
Have you seen the black
issued combat boots?

I will turn your mosques into shopping malls
and build Disney Lands in Tehran
I will paint you as another villain in history
I will take your lands and scar your children
I will bring you liberation

Good Morning Iran

you don't think I've forgotten
about those hostages, do you?
You rejected my banks
what do you mean sovereignty?
You will know freedom

I am morality in a copper casing
I am the thunder of a thousand bombs
I am desert tempest
I am bullet shock
I am the machinery of consumption
I am the bloody talons
I am empire

Good morning Iran

I don't hate you
but I need you to build bombs
I need to sell helicopters
I need to turn the cogs
I need to keep these wheels moving
or my people will start looking around
there must always be another enemy

Good morning Iran

the eagle spreads its wings at dawn

Suburban Meditation

They say man domesticated
the wolf, tamed the beast
just like we claimed the plains
by carving interstate highways
right through the heart of them.

The unnamed creatures hide
in the shadows of brush
but you old wolf, who lay
his head along a master's thigh
who abandoned the call/ the moon

don't you ever miss
the mosses along the rocks
up the mountain sides?
The way fear clings to the air
how a heart's percussion
is the only music a beast needs?

but now, gray whiskered,
you wait for leftovers
slime and scrap from dinner

old wolf, can you
remember the wind?
Can you remember
the way it was before?

But When I Get Clean Baby

the sun will bring us from sleep
a coffee pot on a counter-top
in an apartment we can't recognize
will steep black and bitter

and we will walk the rooms
in our pajamas, sit on the couch
laugh at the memories we've forsaken
muse about old friends on foreign streets

the devil will have forgotten
about us, instead angels will sing
for us, the flowers in the front yard
will bloom for us, the world will be ours

another lost soul will pick up my habit
will wonder Midwestern highways
will trade his words for three am sutras
I will pray for him like others prayed for me

all of the things we told ourselves
at dawn in the squalor we built
will come true and our smiles will
be made of pearls and sugar

and all the apartments we left behind
will be christened again with good souls
who will paint the walls and water the plants
will clean our blood off of the floor boards

when the sun tucks its head beneath
its bed of clouds, we will blow kisses
to the heavens and I will hold you
until the sun welcomes another day

Most Days

at 8 am
I take off my work boots,
lay on my bed and stare
at the smoke stains
left by my grandfather's
cigarettes on the ceiling.

I take a deep breath.

The shift always ends,
how beautiful that
the sun will set too
and I alongside it
will be no more

From the Sidewalk

From the Sidewalk
from the sidewalk
the bay is blue
welcoming
the succubus
of shore town pride

the businessmen
in their suits
are turning this town
into something it's not

a colony of the city
money movers
trade morality
for escalades
and unkept dreams

I remember the waterfront
before they paved it
when the wooden boardwalk
bumped with the nightly tide

when the police
never bothered to bust anyone
for fishing for dinner
and drinking a brew

when west front street
was weird and happening
when you could park
within earshot of the breaking waves
but I see the change

down beer street
where you could always
find a cheap gram
where I first saw
a loaded handgun

where hard times
and section 8
bonded the poor
into a community

they're building condos
for the clean face elite
building high rises
that cost 2000 a month

where were they
when the bayshore
swallowed the coast
when the hurricane
equalized the rich
and poor

in a fifteen foot
storm surge everyone
is afraid
your car is no longer
a status symbol
when it's floating down
the street

suits and hoodies
don't look much different
when you're wading
through four feet of water

from the sidewalk
I watch this town
be swept from the waves
of commercialism

the bodegas of san juan hill
are the next to go
yoga studios and starbucks
will consume the bars then

from the sidewalk
we will wave goodbye
to our homes

John Dorsey

Anything with Feathers

my grandfather taught me
how to shoot at empty beer cans
how to laugh
when things got tough

he hated banks
& doctors

loved chocolate covered cherries
chipped ham & potato chips on sundays

when they chopped off his legs
he started making hook rugs
with ducks in every pattern
until his vision went

even then
sometimes he would close his eyes
real tight

& flap his arms

up & down
up & down

he was donald duck
he was charles lindbergh

he slept with one eye open
in a hospital bed
in the middle of his living room

he squeezed my hand
& told me not to work too hard
it wasn't worth it

he said anything with feathers
could fly.

You Can't Get Blood from the Dead
for Mike James

the sun no longer touches their lips
whatever they knew about love
will remain a mystery.

Greg Before the Fall of the Berlin Wall

in 1984 greg made flowers out of iron & wood
& black ink

molded drama with his bare hands
from clay and the ancient stars
hidden in the city sky

when he drank too much
he could still remember all of the lyrics
to rock you like a hurricane

he could build a trojan horse
for helen of troy
inside his own heart
& tell time by the sun

to keep him
from getting lost.

Annette is Always with You

crazy mark keeps 2 pounds of marijuana
in pringles cans in the cabinet
under his coffeemaker

he keeps his girlfriend on the phone
the entire time he tosses ziplock bags
in my direction

he talks about how her kidneys
failed last week
as if she can't hear him

stopping to cough
while she talks about
which strain helps
with what ails her

they've known each other
since they were kids

he holds the phone tight
against his chest

she's like a patch of daisies
in the florida swamp

if she were to go
the loss would be deeper
than any old can could fill.

The Prettiest Girl in La Junta, Colorado

works the graveyard shift at the loaf n jug
on the corner of north third street
where the county sheriff
comes to get his coffee
every sunday at 2:32 am

she may be the only girl for miles

he tells her a corny joke
& thinks about what
their children might look like

even though she went to school
with his daughter

while she thinks about pricing toilet paper
& off brand soda
& candy bars covered in sugar
or nothing at all
at this time of night

barely out of high school
it still feels like
she hasn't smiled for a generation

hasn't given her heart
to the wind.

The Ballad of Mick Ronson

for maybe the thousandth time
greg mentions that his father
once compared mick ronson to chet baker

one man's rhythm is never the same as another

there isn't enough whiskey here
to keep his sadness out

it's just a good thing they're both dead
or they'd have to sit here
listening to his story too.

Crystal

at 26
you've already been married
to a neo nazi
engaged to an aging hipster
glued to the couch
with taco bell & mom jeans

you say you're into old school punk
rattling off bands i've never heard of
carrying the weight of the world
in every step

you complain about how
it's too cold to stand outside
to smoke a cigarette

you don't need to look at the moonlight
to blame the sky
for everything.

Flashlight Neon Light

greg smiles as he talks about how his daughter
used to run around the house naked as a baby
singing flashlight neon light

all he needs now
is for her to help him
find the funk

but she won't even answer
his calls anymore

flashlight
neon light
red light

it all comes out like a nursery rhyme
reaching back into the past

the night is young
& all he needs
is to find the funk

he's gotta have that funk

that once sang
all the way
into his heart.

Color Theory in the Summer of 1980

on the news all they talked about
was the hostage crisis
ronald reagan looked like john wayne
with whiter teeth or the ghost of gig young
coming back to bring our boys home
from the past

i drank donald duck grapefruit juice
& made war with plastic army men
on our green shag carpet almost every night
until the sun went down

we always freed the hostages
we always waved the flag
unless i got sleepy

like one night
when i spilled juice
all over the tv

red
white
&
blue

suddenly became blue & green bars
on every channel

my father refused to replace it
for at least 10 years

it was perfectly good

by then the hostages really were free
& my men were buried in the backyard
or taken away in garbage bags

the summer sun was sticky
& blood was the color
it was always
supposed to be.

Radio Cities & Number One Records

greg talks about how his friend richard
once shared the stage with alex chilton

mumbling something about the price
that comes with genius

there were no small notes
in the air
that night

only big stars.

Wrestling With the Bear
for Jason Baldinger

it's all a circus babe
winter in pittsburgh
is no joke

the bear will show its teeth
whenever it pleases

just watch out for the high wire
& remember that fried chicken
is even better cold.

The Finger Has Got to Come Off

crazy mark crushes his finger
in the back of a dump truck

instead of going to the hospital
he examines the bone

each angle
like the rings on a tree

each crack
a ridge of undiscovered country

clues to a past
that even he can't quite recall

weeks go by
and the skin
just won't heal

he says he'll have to
cut the meat off himself
before it starts to stink
like a dying animal
left to rot
in the woods.

Jason Baldinger Talks About the Future

he says it's all dick pics & robots
from here on out.

Perpetual Motion

in the 1980's
everything was smooth sailing
except
drugs
aids
starvation
exploding space shuttles
&
the threat of foreign wars

we had miami vice
& a small hole
peeking through the ozone layer
from all of those cans of hairspray

everyone in the trailer park
had a waterbed

our neighbors at the top of the hill
got their kids a chihuahua puppy for christmas

they would take turns tossing it
onto the bed

watching the poor thing
sway back & forth
like a drunken sailor
only a few weeks
after bringing it home
it slid right off the bed

snapping its neck
without even a whimper

rubber ball still firmly in its mouth

as a child's birthday party went on
in full swing in the next room

it was so quiet
that we thought
it was playing a game

& then the youngest neighbor boy
started wailing

as his brother approached the body
with plastic army men
as if it was just some peaceful beast
he had killed in battle

their father covered it up
with a beach towel
as their mother asked us
who wanted cake

& somehow like magic
the decade was over
before it had even really
gotten started.

As Curtis Drives By

crazy mark talks about this woman over in byron
who paid him $100 just to lick her asshole

this morning he was knee deep
in chicken shit
looking for eggs
to get through the winter

but she was too crazy
even for him.

Greg's Mantra

down here bowie & prince are like gods
& if you drink enough cheap bourbon
the stars that light the night sky

will always lead you home

even in a dented minivan.

Detroit Airport in Route to London

12 hours sitting in a plastic chair
across from a p.f. chang's
will turn anyone into a prisoner of war.

Detroit Airport in Route to London #2

the security guards look at you
like you want to be there

as you look out longingly
at the last beautiful girl
you may ever see
eating french fries
out of a suitcase.

Poem for Damian Rucci

wanted men are rare
the rest of us
are everywhere.

At the Venture Hostel

there is a condom machine
in the bathroom

unable to sleep
in the middle bunk

i sit in a shower stall
where babies have probably
been conceived
or left for dead

like all bad decisions

waiting for this night
to disappear.

Beth Saves My Life
for Jason Shelley

at least four times in thirty minutes
a cab driver from morocco
drops me off
at a reading

that feels like an a.a. meeting

a former revolutionary
walks home alone
in the rain

to feed his cats.

Poem for Winston Trew

you pulled your punches
like a man

& left your blood
on the pavement

so others
could find peace.

Victor Clevenger

Poem for My Grandson

congress impeached the president
just hours before your mother
gave birth to you

it's a fact that you
weren't the only red eyes crying
that night   & i

may have just been the happiest
man in town

Southern Un-Hospitality

with the stench of inherited hate
& liquor on their breath

santiago doesn't reply to the provoking

he just lets them say what they want
in the drive-thru lane
because he has only worked
the milkshake machine behind the counter
for three days & he doesn't want
any trouble from the people
in this 'merican city

yet santiago isn't a bad dude
& he doesn't make the milkshakes
taste any different than if
an american had made them
but he's not american

just a good guy lumped into a group
of bad hombres

who have learned first-hand
that there is nothing sweet
about the ignorant tooth
that bites down on the rib bones
of nationalism

2 Lovers on South Aiken Avenue

kissing each other with mouths open wide
mashed together bodies leaning
against a telephone pole

near the closed day care center
on the corner

your hands up her shirt
& hers up yours

i'm certain that you have no clue i'm even there
waking up at 3a.m. on the concrete step
across the street half-hungover
& watching you

thinking about
how i do not feel like a creep

because there is not one single star
in the sky that is dead
& falling

they're all high & holding

watching you two
lust rub & dance

to any pittsburgh street sound
that resembles a tune

What I Didn't Know While Eating Bacon in Jeannette, Pennsylvania

that in only a few short hours
while driving through heavy rain
at sixty miles-per-hour
down a dark illinois hwy
coming home
we'd see at the end of two lusterless headlights
a dead dog lying
in the middle of the road
naturally
it in a motionless state showed
that that we were not the first car to pass by
& in the rearview mirror i could see
that we were not going to be
the last car to pass by either
we were just going to be one of many
passing right through the middle
of a horrible situation
that night
i thought about every dead dog
i'd ever buried
now sitting on wooden stools
somewhere beyond the living
ordering up the first round
for that poor wet bastard's
first night of many
chasing the stars like bones
broken & tossed across
constellations

Three Minutes Late & Out of Luck

rolling slow through a kfc parking lot
in pryor, oklahoma
a young dark-haired girl eating a fried
chicken leg on the other side
of the drive-thru window tells us
we're three minutes late & out of luck
when we try to order food at 10:03 p.m.
you've got to be kidding me!
her compassion like coleslaw's complex
always rejected   horrible
our stomachs now growling like stray dogs
lost in an unfamiliar neighborhood
of vegans   & trash dumpsters
with padlocks

The Color of a Deep Depression

watching the sky fall in thick pieces

like broken blue bricks
or tiny paint chips picked from
a van gogh canvas

who's the monster
that would destroy such masterpieces

have you ever heard it said that
we are all masterpieces

our individuality birthed
by strokes of colored brushes
in the finger pinch
of a powerful someone
splitting their soul in a solarium

it's 9:55 this morning

& i sit here imagining the color
that the water has turned into

all the brushes that created us
sitting in a cracked glass jar on a
windowsill in the sun

i bet it's murky

the color of a deep depression
plummeting down
like raindrops on the thirsty

& that makes sense to me

because most days i feel buried in the dirt
up to the notch in my neck

looking towards the sky
& just taking

what is being given

Lost Man's Candle

standing at the end of a cold day
we think about how it is always here
in some form good for a glow
hanging from a rope
tied to a breeze

it's a lost man's candle
the moon

creating the dull between the trees
branch's shadows like arms reaching out
for a waist to grasp in dance
& we're near

but there is no melody left in our breath
tonight   & there is no whistle
from the lips of the wind either

just the random cries of wild animals
that we've all heard
a thousand times before

as we stood there like fools

too fucking stubborn
to just find

a good path back home

Poem for My Hometown (or, An Abusive Relationship)

your head covered with a white quilt

like a ghost looking off into the distance
i struggle to recognize you anymore

i want to wrap my arms around you, hamilton
& talk like we used to

but you won't reply
because you've let them stitch
your lips shut

for that all mighty dollar
i'm certain that your legs are next

because everyone knows that a nest of hornets
can never grow stronger
if you destroy their existence
right now

Poem for Lora

deep down inside i was secretly prepared for the
reality that our relationship was just another
youngster romance

a couple of crazy kids in the late summer of '96
listening to cake

& going the distance

A Poem About Rose Bushes

independent at seventeen years old
pocketing six-dollars-n-hour
painting bedroom walls
on a saturday afternoon
& afterwards
before the streetlight's flicker
i was drunk again
drifting into a sunday morning
six o'clock awakening
lying on a living room floor
near a window seat
in a low-income housing complex
with an older woman
who shook my shoulder
then led me to a back bedroom
where we ended naked
under heavy covers
sleeping until eleven

that was the first time with her
a month into my senior year
of high school

two weeks removed
from my father's house
& learning
that with nothing to show

the true colors of the petals to come
it's a gamble
to take only a piece of the root
& bury it with assumptions

because twenty-two years ago
i would have sworn to you
that i was growing
a marilyn monroe rose with her
when honestly
i grew nothing more
than a wilted memory lane

Poem for Carlie & Cassie Clevenger

you are both fruit that has finally fallen
& rolled a good distance away
from your mother's tree
  i'm sure
that the orchards in your future will now
be beautiful

Clevenger Painting

when piccard & jones had just flown
the first balloon non-stop around the world
i was working seven days a week
on a job site painting new homes for happy people
with more money than i had
my fingernails stained with minwax
puritan pine & early american
a mixture of shit
smeared on every set of oak cabinets
in platte county missouri spring 1999
nostrils full of hi-build lacquer & dust
ears buzzing huffing stoned
during my lunch breaks talking to tommy
who had spiked hair & a neck tattoo
a hired hand dating my cousin tonya
after he'd done some time in the penitentiary
& i was seven months into my first marriage
at that point working for the family business
so we would joke about how i was doing
a double bit of hard time myself shackled & chained
without the balls & keys to break free
but quite often i'd tell myself
four months past my turning nineteen
that i refuse to stroke myself into a corner
day after day with a thin bristled brush
that had dried up years ago
with someone else's dull
earth toned dreams

I am Legend (or, Poem About Helping My Children Build Valentine's Day Boxes)

the only gun that i own shoots staples
in dreams
i am will smith
navigating through a paper heart
apocalypse

Poem for Madi

in a salina ihop
the first thing i notice is your
long legs

standing on your tippy toes
i bet you can see over the nighttime
into tomorrow

how beautiful
the sound of a distant moan

clouds kissing your neck every night
like a lover

Jay

on a friday just before lunch
you were arrested by the state police
for child pornography
& more

i wonder if they were gentle with you
or if they threatened you
with harm if you ever told a soul
about what they were getting ready
to do to you . . .

the things that change a person forever

Jay #2

after one night in jail
you called michelle
& asked her
to send you money

but she told you no
& to never call again

& i love her
for being strong

you swore to her
that your daughter wasn't
a victim of your actions

goddamn jay

do you realize how stupid
you sound

desperate words rushing
out your mouth like water
through a hole in the bottom
of a boat

that you've packed
your future onto

Jay #3

you went from working in a prison
with us every day

to living in one

walking that razor's edge
& paying rent

with your sins

Jay #4

making excuses as to what
led you down that dark path
to where twelve-year-old girls
became your thing

you blame your mental health

for the reason young girls
argue with their friends
that monsters
are real

Jay #5

sometimes jay
there are no more secrets to hide

some men are nothing more
than wet bones waiting
for the day to be dropped into a hole

& i hope

that your beautiful daughter grows up
with a different
last name

Favorite Couch at the Dorsey Hotel

this couch is fearless
bones once new & shiny
in the summer of '77

when the son of sam still strutted
the streets of queens

this couch is fearless
been this way for forty-two years
with cushions that have sworn to men
they could take a .44 caliber bullet
in the kisser

hot hole burnt through
& through

spit out white stuffing like teeth
into the palm of their hands
before putting it all
into a zipper pocket to share
in stories later

it's craziness
mixed with an unforgettable
scent of cocky

that most can overlook
including me

spread out on top of her
under a plush blanket
with a book of yi sha poems
across my chest

i too
for a moment feel fearless

in my mind
watching an episode of tomorrow play
dancing in the darkness
of tonight

Southern Missouri Hindsight Proverb

on a rusted-out condom vending machine
that hangs on a wall in a bathroom
at a small gas station off highway 67

someone has written

Your Daddy Should Have Bought One Of These

Reggie & The Milkman

in the living room
reggie drunk preaches to the milkman
about living his best life

tells him to get rid
of any & all hate inside of himself

that's tearing at the walls
of his stomach

because one day it may rip open

& how awful would that feel
to have your guts crashing down
to the ground around your bare feet

like a paper sack full of shit
that's been lit on fire

by the flame
of your own bad decisions

This project was made possible, in part, by generous support from the Osage Arts Community.

Osage Arts Community provides temporary time, space and support for the creation of new artistic works in a retreat format, serving creative people of all kinds — visual artists, composers, poets, fiction and nonfiction writers. Located on a 152-acre farm in an isolated rural mountainside setting in Central Missouri and bordered by ¾ of a mile of the Gasconade River, OAC provides residencies to those working alone, as well as welcoming collaborative teams, offering living space and workspace in a country environment to emerging and mid-career artists. For more information, visit us at www.osageac.org

Osage Arts Community

www.ingramcontent.com/pod-product-compliance
Lightning Source LLC
Chambersburg PA
CBHW030337100526
44592CB00010B/724